EMERALD TREE BOAS

BY EMILY ROSE OACHS

BELLWETHER MEDIA • MINNEAPOLIS, MN

EPIC BOOKS are no ordinary books. They burst with intense action, high-speed heroics, and shadows of the unknown. Are you ready for an Epic adventure?

This edition first published in 2014 by Bellwether Media, Inc.

No part of this publication may be reproduced in whole or in part without written permission of the publisher. For information regarding permission, write to Bellwether Media, Inc., Attention: Permissions Department, 5357 Penn Avenue South, Minneapolis, MN 55419.

Library of Congress Cataloging-in-Publication Data

Oachs, Emily Rose, author.
  Emerald Tree Boas / by Emily Rose Oachs.
    pages cm. – (Epic. Amazing Snakes!)
  Summary: "Engaging images accompany information about emerald tree boas. The combination of high-interest subject matter and light text is intended for students in grades 2 through 7"– Provided by publisher.
  Audience: Ages 7-12.
  Includes bibliographical references and index.
  ISBN 978-1-62617-092-6 (hardcover : alk. paper)
  1. Tree boas–Juvenile literature. 2. Camouflage (Biology)–Juvenile literature. I. Title.
  QL666.O63O23 2014
  597.96'7–dc23

                              2013035911

Printed in the United States of America, North Mankato, MN.

TABLE OF CONTENTS

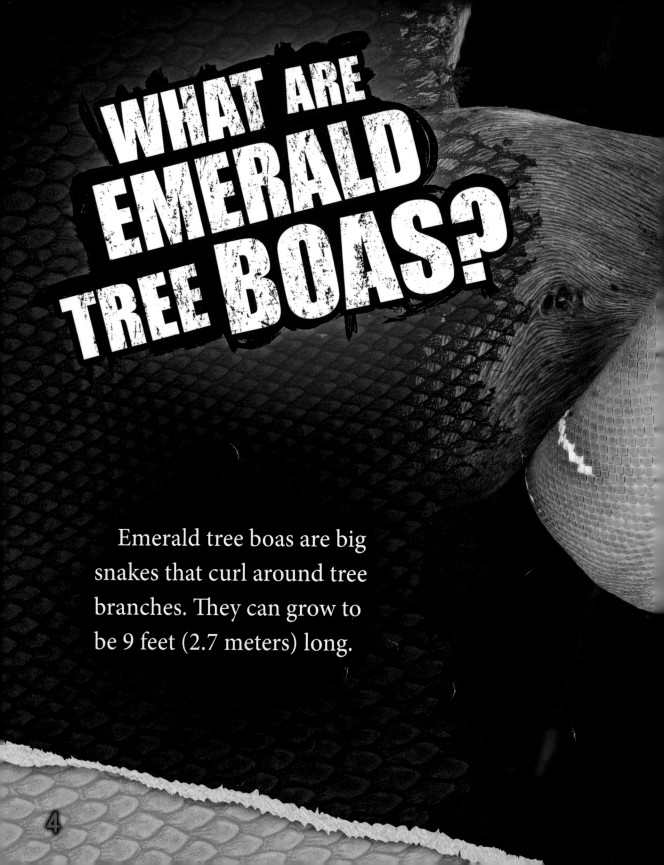

WHAT ARE EMERALD TREE BOAS?

Emerald tree boas are big snakes that curl around tree branches. They can grow to be 9 feet (2.7 meters) long.

5

Emerald tree boas lie very still in the trees. Their bodies **coil** into oval shapes. Their heads rest in the center.

WHERE EMERALD TREE BOAS LIVE

emerald tree boa range =

Emerald tree boas live in the **tropical rain forests** of South America. They spend most of their time in the **canopy**. These snakes slither quickly through the treetops.

Balancing Boas
Strong tails help emerald tree boas balance in the trees.

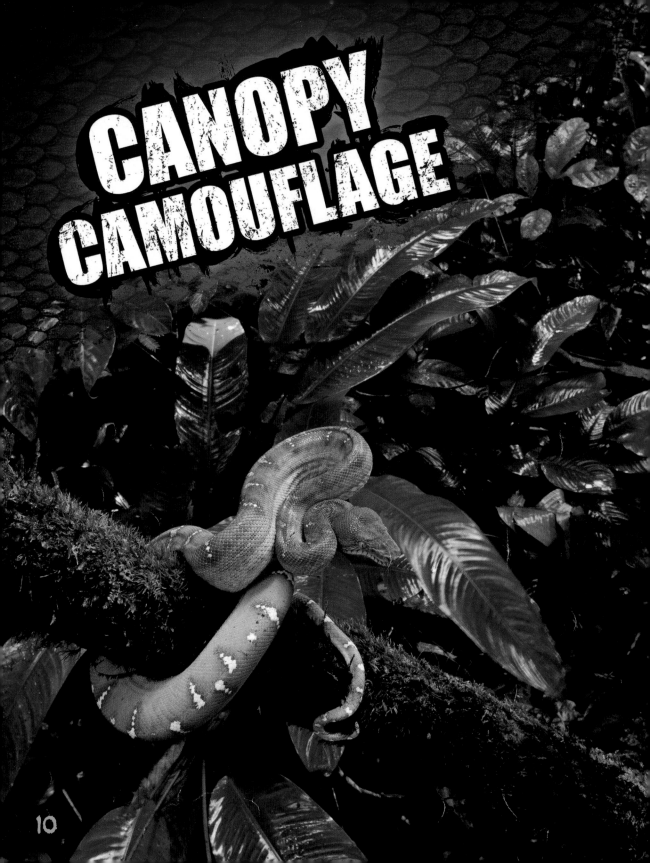

CANOPY CAMOUFLAGE

Young and Bright
Emerald tree boas are born red or orange. They turn green as they get older.

The canopy **camouflages** emerald tree boas. The snakes' bright **scales** blend in with the trees. Their green bodies look like vines. Their small white spots look like sunlight.

Sometimes emerald tree boas cannot hide from **predators**. Eagles swoop into the treetops to hunt these snakes.

HUNTING FOR PREY

Snake Eyes
Emerald tree boas have
pupils that look like slits.
These are the eyes of
night predators.

Emerald tree boas hunt at night. Many tiny
pits surround their mouths. These little holes
sense heat. Pits help boas find lizards, birds,
and rats in the dark.

The snakes snatch **prey** that run under their trees. They hold the prey with their long teeth. Then they wrap their bodies around the animals and squeeze.

Fast Food
Emerald tree boas can even catch birds that are flying!

17

Soon the animals suffocate. The boas stretch their jaws wide. Then they swallow their prey whole!

SPECIES PROFILE

SCIENTIFIC NAME:	*CORALLUS CANINUS*
NICKNAMES:	AMAZON BASIN EMERALD NORTHERN SHIELD EMERALD PARROT SNAKE DOG BOA
AVERAGE SIZE:	4-6 FEET (1.2-1.8 METERS)
HABITAT:	TROPICAL RAIN FORESTS
COUNTRIES:	BOLIVIA, BRAZIL, COLOMBIA, ECUADOR, FRENCH GUIANA, GUYANA, PERU, SURINAME, VENEZUELA
VENOMOUS:	NO
HUNTING METHOD:	CONSTRICTION
COMMON PREY:	BIRDS, LIZARDS, RATS, FROGS, SQUIRRELS, BATS, MONKEYS

GLOSSARY

camouflages—hides an animal or thing by helping it blend in

canopy—the thick covering of leafy branches formed by the tops of trees

coil—to loop around

pits—heat-sensing holes around the mouth; emerald tree boas use pits to hunt for food at night.

predators—animals that hunt other animals for food

prey—animals that are hunted by other animals for food

scales—small plates of skin that cover and protect a snake's body

suffocate—to die from being unable to breathe

tropical rain forests—hot, rainy areas with tall trees

TO LEARN MORE

At the Library

Cherry, Lynne. *The Great Kapok Tree*. San Diego, Calif.: Voyager Books, 1990.

Nichols, Catherine. *Emerald Boas: Rain Forest Undercover*. New York, N.Y.: Bearport Publishing, 2010.

Sexton, Colleen. *Boa Constrictors*. Minneapolis, Minn.: Bellwether Media, 2010.

On the Web

Learning more about emerald tree boas is as easy as 1, 2, 3.

1. Go to www.factsurfer.com.

2. Enter "emerald tree boas" into the search box.

3. Click the "Surf" button and you will see a list of related Web sites.

With factsurfer.com, finding more information is just a click away.

INDEX

The images in this book are reproduced through the courtesy of: Audrey Snider-Bell, front cover, pp. 4-5, 11, 13; Hannamariah, pp. 6-7; Aflo Animal/ Glow Images, pp. 8-9; Biosphoto/ SuperStock, pp. 10-11, 16, 21; Chepe Nicoli, p. 12; Minden Pictures/ SuperStock, pp. 14-15; Dr. Morley Read, p. 15 (top); Dirk Ercken, p. 15 (middle); Gallinago Media, p. 15 (bottom); Biosphoto/ Jany Sauvanet, p. 17; Animals Animals/ SuperStock, pp. 18-19.